KU-662-512

The Illustrated

SUMMONED
BY BELLS

the Horse Tram
West Hill

The Illustrated
SUMMONED
BY BELLS

JOHN BETJEMAN
with paintings and sketches by
HUGH CASSON

JOHN MURRAY

KENT COUNTY LIBRARY

C010151725
821

First published 1960
Reprinted 1960, 1962, 1969, 1977, 1978, 1984 (twice), 1986

This edition with illustrations by Hugh Casson 1989

© John Betjeman 1960, 1966
© Illustrations Hugh Casson 1989

This edition conceived and produced in
association with The Herbert Press

Designed by Pauline Harrison

Set in Monotype (hot-metal) Garamond (156)
by Gloucester Typesetting Services

Published by John Murray (Publishers) Ltd
50 Albemarle Street, London W1X 4BD

All rights reserved
Unauthorised duplication contravenes applicable laws

British Library Cataloguing in Publication Data
Betjeman, John, 1906–1984
   The illustrated summoned by bells
   I. Title   II. Casson. Sir, Hugh, 1910–
821'.912

ISBN 0–7195–4696–6

Printed in Italy by Lito Terrazi

CONTENTS

OTHER VERSE VOLUMES

COLLECTED POEMS
(new reset edition)

UNCOLLECTED POEMS

CHURCH POEMS
Illustrated by John Piper

A RING OF BELLS
Selected and annotated for young
readers by Irene Slade.
Illustrated by Edward Ardizzone

OTHER BOOKS BY OR ABOUT JOHN BETJEMAN

LONDON'S HISTORIC RAILWAY STATIONS

BETJEMAN'S CORNWALL

BETJEMAN'S LONDON
Edited by Pennie Denton

FIRST AND LAST LOVES
(Century Hutchinson paperback)

JOHN BETJEMAN: A LIFE IN PICTURES
Edited by Bevis Hillier

THE FIRST VOLUME OF AUTHORISED BIOGRAPHY

YOUNG BETJEMAN
by Bevis Hillier

Why is this account of some moments in the sheltered life of a middle-class youth not written in prose? The author has gone as near prose as he dare. He chose blank verse, for all but the more hilarious moments, because he found it best suited to brevity and the rapid changes of mood and subject.

He wishes to thank the Proprietors of *Punch* for permission to reprint the Edward James stanzas. He is particularly grateful to his friends John Hanbury Angus Sparrow and Thomas Edward Neil Driberg for going through the manuscript and proofs and making valuable suggestions which have almost always been adopted, and Cecil Roberts for his help. He wishes to thank Messrs. Mears & Stainbank for campanological advice.

West Hill
Highgate

8

CHAPTER I

BEFORE MCMXIV ❧

Middlesex quiet ❧ the big houses and the
small ones ❧ author is told he is an alien ❧
is comforted by a stuffed bear ❧ brickish
Kentish Town seen through leaves of
Highgate ❧ an altercation at an auction
bridge party ❧ centipedes and glomeridae ❧
an unpleasant nursemaid ❧ her violence and
rather peculiar methods ❧

Here on the southern slope of Highgate Hill
Red squirrels leap the hornbeams. Still I see
Twigs and serrated leaves against the sky.
The sunny silence was of Middlesex.
Once a Delaunay-Belleville crawling up
West Hill in bottom gear made such a noise
As drew me from my dream-world out to watch
That early motor-car attempt the steep.
But mostly it was footsteps, rustling leaves,
And blackbirds fluting over miles of Heath.

　　　Then Millfield Lane looked like a Constable
And all the grassy hillocks spoke of Keats.
Mysterious gravel drives to hidden wealth
Wound between laurels – mighty Caenwood Towers
And Grand Duke Michael's house and Holly Lodge.

　　　But what of us in our small villa row
Who gazed into the Burdett-Coutts estate?

I knew we were a lower, lesser world
Than that remote one of the carriage-folk
Who left their cedars and brown garden walls
In care of servants. I could also tell
That we were slightly richer than my friends,
The family next door: we owned a brougham
And they would envy us our holidays.
In fact it was the mother there who first
Made me aware of insecurity
When war was near: "Your name is German, John" –
But I had always thought that it was Dutch . . .
That tee-jay-ee, that fatal tee-jay-ee
Which I have watched the hesitating pens
Of Government clerks and cloakroom porters funk.
I asked my mother. "No," she said, "it's Dutch;
Thank God you're English on your mother's side."
O happy, happy Browns and Robinsons!

     Safe were those evenings of the pre-war world
When firelight shone on green linoleum;
I heard the church bells hollowing out the sky,
Deep beyond deep, like never-ending stars,
And turned to Archibald, my safe old bear,
Whose woollen eyes looked sad or glad at me,
Whose ample forehead I could wet with tears,
Whose half-moon ears received my confidence,
Who made me laugh, who never let me down.
I used to wait for hours to see him move,
Convinced that he could breathe. One dreadful day
They hid him from me as a punishment:
Sometimes the desolation of that loss

Comes back to me and I must go upstairs
To see him in the sawdust, so to speak,
Safe and returned to his idolator.
    Safe, in a world of trains and buttered toast
Where things inanimate could feel and think,
Deeply I loved thee, 31 West Hill!
At that hill's foot did London then begin,
With yellow horse-trams clopping past the planes
To grey-brick nonconformist Chetwynd Road
And on to Kentish Town and barking dogs

Costers' Carts Kentish Town.

31 West Hill . N.6   HC.

12

And costers' carts and crowded grocers' shops
And Daniels' store, the local Selfridge's,
The Bon Marché, the Electric Palace, slums
That thrilled me with their smells of poverty –
Till, safe once more, we gained the leafy slope
And buttered toast and 31 West Hill.
Here from my eyrie, as the sun went down,
I heard the old North London puff and shunt,
Glad that I did not live in Gospel Oak.

"A diamond," "A heart," "No trumps," "Two spades" –
Happy and tense they played at Auction Bridge:
Two tables in the drawing-room for friends
From terra-cotta flats on Muswell Hill

And nearer Brookfield Mansions: cigarettes
And 'Votes for Women' ashtrays, mauve and green.
I watched the players, happy to be quiet
Till someone nice was dummy who would talk –
A talk soon drowned . . . "If you'd finessed my heart
And played your diamond . . ." "If I'd had the lead
I might have done." "Well, length is strength, you know."
"Not when your partner's sitting on the ace."
Did they, I wonder, leave us in a huff
After those hot post-mortems? All I knew
Were silks and bits of faintly scented fur
On ladies vaguely designated 'aunts'
Who came on second Thursdays to At Homes.
    The sunlit weeks between were full of maids:
Sarah, with orange wig and horsy teeth,
Was so bad-tempered that she scarcely spoke;
Maud was my hateful nurse who smelt of soap
And forced me to eat chewy bits of fish,
Thrusting me back to babyhood with threats
Of nappies, dummies and the feeding bottle.
She rubbed my face in messes I had made
And was the first to tell me about Hell,
Admitting she was going there herself.
Sometimes, thank God, they left me all alone
In our small patch of garden in the front,
With clinker rockery and London Pride
And barren lawn and lumps of yellow clay
As mouldable as smelly Plasticine.
I used to turn the heavy stones to watch
The shiny red and waiting centipede

Evening Party
31 West Hill

15

Which darted out of sight; the woodlouse slow
And flat; the other greyish-bluey kind
Which rolled into a ball till I was gone
Out of the gate to venture down the hill.
  "You're late for dinner, John." I feel again
That awful feeling, fear confused with thrill,
As I would be unbuttoned, bent across
Her starchy apron, screaming "Don't – Maud – don't!"
Till dissolution, bed and kindly fur
Of agéd, uncomplaining Archibald.

Archibald.

CHAPTER II

THE DAWN OF GUILT ✎

The author's father ✎ his interest in antiques
✎ factory in Pentonville Road ✎ foundation
of the family fortunes ✎ office and show-
rooms ✎ attitude of the wholesaler to the
retailer ✎ author expected to carry on family
business ✎ its employees ✎ author's
preference for poetry ✎ early attempts at
writing it ✎ its weakness ✎ inspiration from
Highgate ✎ and from 'The Hopeless Dawn'
✎ disappointment of father ✎

My dear deaf father, how I loved him then
Before the years of our estrangement came!
The long calm walks on twilit evenings
Through Highgate New Town to the cinema:
The expeditions by North London trains
To dim forgotten stations, wooden shacks
On oil-lit flimsy platforms among fields
As yet unbuilt-on, deep in Middlesex . . .
We'd stand in dark antique shops while he talked,
Holding his deaf-appliance to his ear,
Lifting the ugly mouthpiece with a smile
Towards the flattered shopman. Most of all
I think my father loved me when we went
In early-morning pipe-smoke on the tram
Down to the Angel, visiting the Works.
"Fourth generation – yes, this is the boy."

North London Trains

The smell of sawdust still brings back to me
The rambling workshops high on Pentonville,
Built over gardens to White Lion Street,
Clicking with patents of the family firm
Founded in 1820. When you rang
The front-door bell a watchful packer pulled
A polished lever twenty yards away,
And this released the catch into a world
Of shining showrooms full of secret drawers
And Maharajahs' dressing-cases.

                                    Hushed
Be thy green hilltop, handsome Highbury!
Stilled be the traffic roar of Upper Street!
Flash shop-fronts, masts and neon signs, drop off
The now-encumbered houses! O return,
Straw-smelling mornings, to old Islington!
A hint of them still hung about the Works
From the past days of our prosperity –
A hint of them in medals, photographs
And stockrooms heavy with the Tantalus
On which the family fortune had been made.

the "B" Quality Tantalus
Well finished in oak, walnut or mahogany.

The Alexandra Palace patent lock,
The Betjemann device for hansom cabs,
Patents exhibited in '51,
Improvements on them shown in '62,
The Betjemann trolley used in coffee-rooms,
The inlaid brass, the figured rosewood box,
The yellow satinwood, the silverware –
What wealth the money from them once had brought
To fill the hot-house half-way up the stairs
With red begonias; what servants' halls;
What terrace houses and what carriage-drives!

G. Betjemann & Sons – Showrooms & Manufactᵃ

Bang through the packing-room! Then up a step:
"Be careful, Master John," old William called.
Over the silversmiths' uneven floor
I thought myself a fast electric train,
First stop the silver-plating shop (no time
To watch the locksmiths' and engravers' work):
For there in silence Buckland used to drop
Dull bits of metal into frothing tanks
And bring them out all gold or silver bright –
He'd turn a penny into half-a-crown.
Though he but seldom spoke, yet he and I

FOUNDED 1820

PEARS

6-44 Pentonville Rd London N.

The G. Betjemann Manufactory. Pentonville Road.

Worked there as one. He let me seem to work.
The cabinet-makers' shop, all belts and wheels
And whining saws, would thrill me with the scream
Of tortured wood, starting a blackened plank
Under the cruel plane and coming out
Sweet-scented, pink and smooth and richly grained;
While in a far-off shed, caressingly,
French-polishers, all whistling different tunes,
With reeking swabs would rub the coloured woods,
Bringing the figured surfaces to light;
Dark whirling walnut, deep and deeper brown,
And rare mahogany's pressed butterflies.
Beside the timber yard, a favourite hut
Encased the thumping heartbeat of the Works,
An old gas-engine smelling strong of oil.
Its mighty wheel revolved a leather belt
Which, turning lesser wheels and lesser belts,
Spread like a drawing by Heath Robinson
Through all the rambling length of wooden sheds.

When lunch-time brought me hopes of ginger-beer
I'd meet my father's smile as there he stood
Among his clerks, with pens behind their ears,
In the stern silence of the counting-house;
And he, perhaps not ready to go out,
Would leave me to explore some upper rooms –
One full of ticking clocks, one full of books;
And once I found a dusty drawing-room,
Completely furnished, where long years ago
My great-grandfather lived above his work
Before he moved to sylvan Highbury.
But in the downstair showrooms I could find
No link between the finished articles
And all the clatter of the factory.
The Works in Birmingham, I knew, made glass;
The stoneworks in Torquay made other things . . .
But what did *we* do? This I did not know,
Nor ever wished to – to my father's grief.

O Mappin, Webb, Asprey and Finnigan!
You polished persons on the retail side –
Old Mag Tags, Paulines and Old Westminsters –
Why did I never take to you? Why now
When, staying in a quiet country house,
I see an onyx ashtray of the firm,
Or in my bedroom, find the figured wood
Of my smooth-sliding dressing-table drawers
Has got a look about it of the Works,
Does my mind flinch so?

                      Partly it is guilt:
'Following in Father's footsteps' was the theme

Of all my early childhood. With what pride
He introduced me to old gentlemen,
Pin-striped commercial travellers of the firm
And tall proprietors of Bond Street shops.
With joy he showed me old George Betjeman's book.
(He was a one-'n' man before the craze
For all things German tacked another 'n'):
'December eighteen seven. Twelve and six –
For helping brother William with his desk.'
Uninteresting then it seemed to me,
Uninteresting still. Slow walks we took
On sunny afternoons to great-great-aunts
In tall Italianate houses: Aberdeen Park,
Hillmarton Road and upper Pooter-land,
Short gravel drives to steepish flights of steps
And stained-glass windows in a purple hall,
A drawing-room with stands of potted plants,
Lace curtains screening other plants beyond.
"Fourth generation – yes, this is the boy."
        Partly my guilt is letting down the men –
William our coachman who, turned chauffeur, still
Longed for his mare and feared the motor-car
Which he would hiss at, polishing its sides;
Bradshaw and Pettit of the lathe and plane;
Fieldhouse and Lovely, and the old and bent
With wire-framed spectacles and aproned knees;
The young apprentices old custom called,
Indentures done, to passing-out parade
Down a long alley formed among the men
Beating on bits of metal. How they all

"Tall Italianate houses"

Trusted that I would fill my father's place!
"The Guv'nor's looking for you, Master John . . ."
"Well now, my boy, I want your solemn word
To carry on the firm when I am gone:
Fourth generation, John – they'll look to you.
They're artist-craftsmen to their fingertips . . .
Go on creating beauty!"
                        What is beauty?
Here, where I write, the green Atlantic bursts
In cannonades of white along Pentire.
There's beauty here. There's beauty in the slate
And granite smoothed by centuries of sea,
And washed to life as rain and spray bring out
Contrasting strata higher up the cliff,
But none to me in polished wood and stone

Tortured by Father's craftsmen into shapes
To shine in Asprey's showrooms under glass,
A Maharajah's eyeful.
                                    For myself,
I knew as soon as I could read and write
That I must be a poet. Even today,
When all the way from Cambridge comes a wind
To blow the lamps out every time they're lit,
I know that I must light mine up again.

    My first attraction was to tripping lines;
Internal rhyming, as in Shelley's 'Cloud',
Seemed then perfection. 'O'er' and 'ere' and 'e'en'
Were words I liked to use. My father smiled:
"And how's our budding bard? Let what you write
Be funny, John, and be original."
Secretly proud, I showed off merrily.
But certain as the stars above the twigs
And deeply fearful as the pealing bells
And everlasting as the racing surf
Blown back upon itself in Polzeath Bay,
My urge was to encase in rhythm and rhyme
The things I saw and felt (I could not *think*).

    And so, at sunset, off to Hampstead Heath
I went with pencil and with writing-pad
And stood tip-toe upon a little hill,
Awaiting inspiration from the sky.
"Look! there's a poet!", people might exclaim
On footpaths near. The muse inspired my pen:
The sunset tipped with gold St. Michael's church,
Shouts of boys bathing came from Highgate Ponds,

The elms that hid the houses of the great
Rustled with mystery, and dirt-grey sheep
Grazed in the foreground; but the lines of verse
Came out like parodies of *A & M*.
　　　The gap between my feelings and my skill
Was so immense, I wonder I went on.
A stretch of heather seen at Haslemere
And 'Up the airy mountain' (Allingham)
Merged in the magic of my Highgate pen:

> When the moors are pink with heather
> 　　When the sky's as blue as the sea,
> Marching all together
> 　　Come fairy folk so wee.

Hampstead Heath

My goodness me! It seemed perfection then –
The brilliance of the rhymes A B, A B!
The vastness and the daintiness combined!
The second verse was rather less inspired:

> Some in green and some in red
>> And some with a violet plume,
> And a little cap on each tiny head
>> Watching the bright white moon.

I copied out the lines into a book,
A leather-bound one given me for verse
And stamped with my initials. There it stood
On the first page, that poem – a reproach.

In later years I falsified the date
To make it seem that I was only seven,
Not eight, when these weak stanzas were composed.
   The gap from feeling to accomplishment!
In Highgate days that gap was yawning wide,
But awe and mystery were everywhere,
Most in the purple dark of thin St. Anne's:
Down Fitzroy Park what unimagined depths
Of glade led on to haunts of Robin Hood
(Never a real favourite of mine).
A special Tube train carried Archibald
Northward to Merton, south to Millfield Lane.
A silver blight that made my blood run cold
Hung on a grey house by the cemetery –
So that for years I only liked red brick.
The turrets on the chapel for the dead
And Holly Village with its prickly roofs
Against the sky were terrifying shapes.
"Dong!" went the distant cemetery bell
And chilled for good the east side of the hill
And all things east of me. But in the west
Were health and sunshine, bumps on Hampstead Heath,
Friends, comfort, railways, brandy-balls and grass;
And west of westward, somewhere, Cornwall lay.
   Once when my father took me to the Tate
We stood enraptured by 'The Hopeless Dawn',
The picture first to move me. Twenty times,
They told me, had Frank Bramley watched the flame
Expiring in its candlestick before
He put it down on canvas. Guttering there,

It symbolized the young wife's dying hope
And the old mother's – gazing out to sea:
The meal upon the table lay prepared
But no good man to eat it: through the panes,
An angry sea below the early light
Tossed merciless, as I had seen the waves
In splendid thunder over Greenaway
Send driftwood shooting up the beach as though
Great planks were light as paper. "Put it down!
Translate the picture into verse, my boy,
And here's your opening –

> Through the humble cottage window
> Streams the early dawn."

The lines my father gave me sounded well;
But how continue them? How make a rhyme?

> O'er the tossing bay of Findow
>   In the mournful morn.

With rising hopes I sought a gazetteer –
Findochty, Findon, Finglas, Finistère –
Alas! no Findow . . . and the poem died.
    Atlantic rollers bursting in my ears,
And pealing church-bells and the puff of trains,
The sight of sailing clouds, the smell of grass –
Were always calling out to me for words.
I caught at them and missed and missed again.
'Catch hold,'' my father said, ''catch hold like this!'',
Trying to teach me how to carpenter,
"Not *that* way, boy! When will you ever learn?'' –
I dug the chisel deep into my hand.
"Shoot!'' said my father, helping with my gun
And aiming at the rabbit – "Quick, boy, fire!''
But I had not released the safety-catch.
I was a poet. That was why I failed.

32

My faith in this chimera brought an end
To all my father's hopes. In later years,
Now old and ill, he asked me once again
To carry on the firm, I still refused.
And now when I behold, fresh-published, new,
A further volume of my verse, I see
His kind grey eyes look woundedly at mine,
I see his workmen seeking other jobs,
And that red granite obelisk that marks
The family grave in Highgate Cemetery
Points an accusing finger to the sky.

Family Grave Highgate Cemetery.

CHAPTER III

HIGHGATE ✎

First love affair and tea at the spacious house
of the beloved ✎ kindergarten foes ✎
interview with the Headmaster and
admittance to Highgate Junior School ✎
suspected of being a German spy ✎
unsavoury adventure walking back from
school ✎ early tastes in poetry ✎ the
American master, Mr. Eliot, and the enigma
of his opinion of author's poems ✎

O Peggy Purey-Cust, how pure you were:
My first and purest love, Miss Purey-Cust!
Satchel on back I hurried up West Hill
To catch you on your morning walk to school,
Your nanny with you and your golden hair
Streaming like sunlight. Strict deportment made
You hold yourself erect and every step
Bounced up and down as though you walked on springs.
Your ice-blue eyes, your lashes long and light,
Your sweetly freckled face and turned-up nose
So haunted me that all my loves since then
Have had a look of Peggy Purey-Cust.
Along the Grove, what happy, happy steps
Under the limes I took to Byron House,
And blob-work, weaving, carpentry and art,
Walking with you; and with what joy returned.
Wendy you were to me in *Peter Pan*,

The Little Match Girl in Hans Andersen –
But I would rescue you before you died.
And once you asked me to your house to tea:
It seemed a palace after 31 –
The lofty entrance hall, the flights of stairs,
The huge expanse of sunny drawing-room,
Looking for miles across the chimney-pots
To spired St. Pancras and the dome of Paul's;
And there your mother from a sofa smiled.
After that tea I called and called again,
But Peggy was not in. She was away;
She wasn't well. *House of the Sleeping Winds*,
My favourite book with whirling art-nouveau
And Walter Crane-ish colour plates, I brought
To cheer her sick-bed. It was taken in.
Weeks passed and passed . . . and then it was returned.
Oh gone for ever, Peggy Purey-Cust!

  And at that happy school in Byron House
Only one harbinger of future woe
Came to me in those far, sun-gilded days –
Gold with the hair of Peggy Purey-Cust –
Two other boys (my rivals, I suppose)
Came suddenly round a corner, caught my arms
And one, a treacherous, stocky little Scot,
Winded me with a punch and "Want some more?"
He grunted when I couldn't speak for pain.
Why did he do it? Why that other boy,
Who hitherto had been a friend of mine,
Was his accomplice I could not divine,
Nor ever have done. But those fatal two

Continued with me to another school –
Avernus by the side of Highgate Hill.

    Let those who have such memories recollect
Their sinking dread of going back to school.
I well remember mine. I see again
The great headmaster's study lined with books
Where somewhere, in a corner, there were canes.
He wrapped his gown, the great headmaster did,
About himself, chucked off his mortar-board
And, leaning back, said: "Let's see what you know,
How many half-crowns are there in a pound?"
I didn't know. I couldn't even guess.
My poor fond father, hearing nothing, smiled;
The gold clock ticked; the waiting furniture
Shone like a colour plate by H. M. Brock . . .

No answer – and the great headmaster frown'd;
But let me in to Highgate Junior School.

In late September, in the conker time,
When Poperinghe and Zillebeke and Mons
Boomed with five-nines, large sepia gravures
Of French, Smith-Dorrien and Haig were given
Gratis with each half-pound of Brooke Bond tea.
A neighbour's son had just been killed at Ypres;
Another had been wounded. *Rainbow* came
On Wednesdays – with the pranks of Tiger Tim,
And Bonnie Bluebell and her magic gloves.
'Your Country needs you!' serious Kitchener
Commanded from the posters. Up West Hill
I walked red-capped and jacketed to school,
A new boy much too early: school at nine,
And here I was outside at half-past eight.

I see the asphalt slope and smell again
The sluggish, sour, inadequate latrines.
I watch the shrubbery shake as, leaping out,
Come my two enemies of Byron House,
But now red-capped and jacketed like me:

"Betjeman's a German spy –
  Shoot him down and let him die:
  Betjeman's a German spy,
  A German spy, a German spy."

They danced around me and their merry shouts
Brought other merry newcomers to see.
    Walking from school is a consummate art:
Which routes to follow to avoid the gangs,
Which paths to find that lead, circuitous,
To leafy squirrel haunts and plopping ponds,
For dreams of Archibald and Tiger Tim;
Which hiding-place is safe, and when it is;
What time to leave to dodge the enemy.
I only once was trapped. I knew the trap –
I heard it in their tones: "Walk back with us."
I knew they weren't my friends; but that soft voice
Wheedled me from my route to cold Swain's Lane.
There in a holly bush they threw me down,
Pulled off my shorts, and laughed and ran away;
And, as I struggled up, I saw grey brick,
The cemetery railings and the tombs.
    See the rich elms careering down the hill –
Full billows rolling into Holloway;
In the tall classroom hear again the drone

Swains Lane. Highgate.   H

Of multiplication tables chanted out;
Recall how Kelly stood us in a ring:
"Three sevens, then add eight, and take away
Twelve; what's the answer?" Hesitation then
Meant shaking by the shoulders till we cried.
Deal out again the dog-eared poetry books
Where Hemans, Campbell, Longfellow and Scott
Mixed their dim lights with Edgar Allan Poe
(Who 'died of dissipation', said the notes).
"And what is dissipation, please, Miss Long?"
Its dreadfulness so pleased me that I learned
'The Bells' by heart, but all the time preferred
'Casabianca' and 'The Hesperus'
As poetry, and Campbell's 'Soldier's Dream'.
I couldn't see why Shakespeare was admired;
I thought myself as good as Campbell now
And very nearly up to Longfellow;
And so I bound my verse into a book,
The Best of Betjeman, and handed it
To one who, I was told, liked poetry –
The American master, Mr. Eliot.
That dear good man, with Prufrock in his head
And Sweeney waiting to be agonized,
I wonder what he thought? He never says
When now we meet, across the port and cheese.
He looks the same as then, long, lean and pale,
Still with the slow deliberating speech
And enigmatic answers. At the time
A boy called Jelly said "He thinks they're bad" –
But he himself is still too kind to say.

CHAPTER IV

CORNWALL IN CHILDHOOD ✎

The London and South Western Railway's
longest run ✎ Cornish creatures of the night
✎ empty beach before breakfast ✎ seaside
friends ✎ cliff climbing ✎ Mr. Oakley's
treasure hunts ✎ Joan Larkworthy's escape
✎ class distinction ✎ noise of waves ✎ sea
smells ✎ a shopping expedition to
Padstow ✎

Come, Hygiene, goddess of the growing boy,
    I here salute thee in Sanatogen!
    Anaemic girls need Virol, but for me
Be Scott's Emulsion, rusks, and Mellin's Food,
Cod-liver oil and malt, and for my neck
Wright's Coal Tar Soap, Euthymol for my teeth.
Come, friends, of Hygiene, Electricity
And those young twins, Free Thought and clean Fresh Air:
Attend the long express from Waterloo
That takes us down to Cornwall. Tea-time shows
The small fields waiting, every blackthorn hedge
Straining inland before the south-west gale.
The emptying train, wind in the ventilators,
Puffs out of Egloskerry to Tresméer
Through minty meadows, under bearded trees
And hills upon whose sides the clinging farms
Hold Bible Christians. Can it really be

That this same carriage came from Waterloo?
On Wadebridge station what a breath of sea
Scented the Camel valley! Cornish air,
Soft Cornish rains, and silence after steam . . .
As out of Derry's stable came the brake
To drag us up those long, familiar hills,
Past haunted woods and oil-lit farms and on
To far Trebetherick by the sounding sea.
        Oh what a host of questions in me rose:
Were spring tides here or neap? And who was down?
Had Mr. Rosevear built himself a house?
Was there another wreck upon Doom Bar?
The carriage lamps lit up the pennywort
And fennel in the hedges of the lane;
Huge slugs were crawling over slabs of slate;
Then, safe in bed, I watched the long-legg'd fly
With red transparent body tap the walls
And fizzle in the candle flame and drag
Its poisonous-looking abdomen away

Bungalow . St Trebetherick .

43

To somewhere out of sight and out of mind,
While through the open window came the roar
Of full Atlantic rollers on the beach.

     Then before breakfast down toward the sea
I ran alone, monarch of miles of sand,
Its shining stretches satin-smooth and vein'd.
I felt beneath bare feet the lugworm casts
And walked where only gulls and oyster-catchers
Had stepped before me to the water's edge.
The morning tide flowed in to welcome me,
The fan-shaped scallop shells, the backs of crabs,
The bits of driftwood worn to reptile shapes,
The heaps of bladder-wrack the tide had left
(Which, lifted up, sent sandhoppers to leap
In hundreds round me) answered "Welcome back!"
Along the links and under cold Bray Hill
Fresh water pattered from an iris marsh

And drowned the golf-balls on its stealthy way
Over the slates in which the elvers hid,
And spread across the beach. I used to stand,
A speculative water engineer –
Here I would plan a dam and there a sluice
And thus divert the stream, creating lakes,
A chain of locks descending to the sea.
Inland I saw, above the tamarisks,
From various villas morning breakfast smoke
Which warned me then of mine; so up the lane
I wandered home contented, full of plans,
Pulling a length of pink convolvulus
Whose blossoms, almost as I picked them, died.

     Bright as the morning sea those early days!
Though there were tears, and sand thrown in my eyes,
And punishments and smells of mackintosh,
Long barefoot climbs to fetch the morning milk,

Golf Course - St Enodoc.

Terrors from hissing geese and angry shouts,
Slammed doors and waitings and a sense of dread,
Still warm as shallow sea-pools in the sun
And welcoming to me the girls and boys.
    Wet rocks on which our bathing dresses dried:
Small coves, deserted in our later years
For more adventurous inlets down the coast:
Paralysis when climbing up the cliff –
Too steep to reach the top, too far to fall,
Tumbling to death in seething surf below,
A ledge just wide enough to lodge one's foot,
A sea-pink clump the only thing to clutch,
Cold wave-worn slate so mercilessly smooth
And no one near and evening coming on –

46

Till Ralph arrived: "Now put your left foot here.
Give us your hand" . . . and back across the years
I swing to safety with old friends again.
Small seem they now, those once tremendous cliffs,
Diminished now those joy-enclosing bays.

     Sweet were the afternoons of treasure-hunts.
We searched in pairs and lifted after showers
The diamond-sparkling sprays of tamarisk:
Their pendent raindrops would release themselves
And soak our shirt-sleeves. Then upon the links
Under a tee-box lay a baffling clue:
A foursome puffing past the sunlit hedge
With rattling golf bags; all the singing grass
Busy with crickets and blue butterflies;

The burnet moths, the unresponsive sheep
Seemed maddeningly indifferent to our plight . . .
"Oh, hurry up, man: why, we're third from last."
And in the Oakleys' garden after tea
Of splits and cream under old apple boughs,
With high tide offering prospects of a bathe,
The winners had their prizes. Once I won –
But that was an unfortunate affair:
My mother set the clues and I, the host,
Knew well the likely workings of her mind.

    Do you remember, Joan, the awkward time
When we were non-co-operative at sports,
Refusing to be organized in heats?
And when at last we were, and had to race
Out to low-tide line and then back again,
A chocolate biscuit was the only prize?
I laughed. Miss Tunstall sent me home to bed.
You laughed, but not so loudly, and escaped.

    That was the summer Audrey, Joc and I
And all the rest of us were full of hope:
"Miss Usher's coming." Who Miss Usher was,
And why she should be coming, no one asked.
She came, a woman of the open air,
Swarthy and in Girl Guide-y sort of clothes:
How nice she was to Audrey and to Joc,
How *very* nice to Biddy and to Joan . . .
But somehow, somehow, not so nice to me.
"I *love* Miss Usher", Audrey said. "Don't you?"
"Oh yes," I answered. "So do I," said Joc
"We vote Miss Usher topping. Itchicoo!"

What was it I had done? Made too much noise?
Increased Miss Tunstall's headache? Disobeyed?
After Miss Usher had gone home to Frant,
Miss Tunstall took me quietly to the hedge:
"Now shall I tell you what Miss Usher said
About you, John?" "Oh please, Miss Tunstall, do!"
"She said you were a common little boy."

    Childhood is measured out by sounds and smells
And sights, before the dark of reason grows.
Ears! Hear again the wild sou'westers whine!
Three days on end would the September gale
Slam at our bungalows; three days on end
Rattling cheap doors and making tempers short.
It mattered not, for then enormous waves
House-high rolled thunderous on Greenaway,
Flinging up spume and shingle to the cliffs.

Unmoved amid the foam, the cormorant
Watched from its peak. In all the roar and swirl
The still and small things gained significance.
Somehow the freckled cowrie would survive
And prawns hang waiting in their watery woods;
Deep in the noise there was a core of peace;
Deep in my heart a warm security.

     Nose! Smell again the early morning smells:
Congealing bacon and my father's pipe;
The after-breakfast freshness out of doors
Where sun had dried the heavy dew and freed
Acres of thyme to scent the links and lawns;
The rotten apples on our shady path
Where blowflies settled upon squashy heaps,
Intent and gorging; at the garden gate
Reek of Solignum on the wooden fence;
Mint round the spring, and fennel in the lane,

And honeysuckle wafted from the hedge;
The Lynams' cess-pool like a body-blow;
Then, clean, medicinal and cold – the sea.
"Breathe in the ozone, John. It's iodine."
But which is iodine and which is drains?
Salt and hot sun on rubber water-wings . . .
Home to the luncheon smell of Irish stew
And washing-up stench from the kitchen sink
Because the sump is blocked. The afternoons
Brought coconut smell of gorse; at Mably's farm
Sweet scent of drying cowdung; then the moist
Exhaling of the earth in Shilla woods –
First earth encountered after days of sand.
Evening brought back the gummy smell of toys
And fishy stink of glue and Stickphast paste,
And sleep inside the laundriness of sheets.

  Eyes! See again the rock-face in the lane,
Years before tarmac and the motor-car.
Across the estuary Stepper Point
Stands, still unquarried, black against the sun;

On its Atlantic face the cliffs fall sheer.
Look down into the weed world of the lawn –
The devil's-coach-horse beetle hurries through,
Lifting its tail up as I bar the way
To further flowery jungles.
                              See once more
The Padstow ferry, worked by oar and sail,
Her outboard engine always going wrong,
Ascend the slippery quay's up-ended slate,
The sea-weed hanging from the harbour wall.
Hot was the pavement under, as I gazed

Marine Stores. Padstow

At lanterns, brass, rope and ships' compasses
In the marine-store window on the quay.
The shoe-shop in the square was cool and dark.
The Misses Quintrell, fancy stationers,
Had most to show me – dialect tales in verse
Published in Truro (Netherton and Worth)
And model lighthouses of serpentine.
Climb the steep hill to where that belt of elm
Circles the town and church tower, reached by lanes
Whose ferny ramparts shelter toadflax flowers
And periwinkles. See hydrangeas bloom
In warm back-gardens full of fuchsia bells.

To the returning ferry soon draws near
Our own low bank of sand-dunes; then the walk
Over a mile of quicksand evening-cold.
        It all is there, excitement for the eyes,
Imagined ghosts on unfrequented roads
Gated and winding up through broom and gorse
Out of the parish, on to who knows where?
What pleasure, as the oil-lamp sparkled gold
On cut-glass tumblers and the flip of cards,
To feel protected from the night outside:
Safe Cornish holidays before the storm!

CHAPTER V

PRIVATE SCHOOL ✎

A skilful lie ✎ doing one's bit ✎ a bicycle
ride through North Oxford ✎ Crick Road
and retired professors ✎ exploring churches
with Ronnie Wright ✎ influence of water-
colour plates ✎ admiration of Gothic ✎
Gerald Haynes, the good schoolmaster ✎
a river expedition ✎

Percival Mandeville, the perfect boy,
  Was all a schoolmaster could wish to see –
  Upright and honourable, good at games,
Well-built, blue-eyed; a sense of leadership
Lifted him head and shoulders from the crowd.
His work was good. His written answers, made
In a round, tidy and decided hand,
Pleased the examiners. His open smile
Enchanted others. He could also frown
On anything unsporting, mean or base,
Unworthy of the spirit of the school
And what it stood for. Oh the dreadful hour
When once upon a time he frowned on me!
Just what had happened I cannot recall –
Maybe some bullying in the dormitory;
But well I recollect his warning words:
"I'll fight you, Betjeman, you swine, for that,
Behind the bike shed before morning school."

So all the previous night I spewed with fear.
I could not box: I greatly dreaded pain.
A recollection of the winding punch
Jack Drayton once delivered, blows and boots
Upon the bum at Highgate Junior School,
All multiplied by X from Mandeville,
Emptied my bladder. Silent in the dorm
I cleaned my teeth and clambered into bed.
Thin seemed pyjamas and inadequate
The regulation blankets once so warm.
"What's up?" "Oh, nothing." I expect they knew . . .
And, in the morning, cornflakes, bread and tea,
Cook's Farm Eggs and a spoon of marmalade,
Which heralded the North and Hillard hours
Of Latin composition, brought the post.
Breakfast and letters! Then it was a flash
Of hope, escape and inspiration came:
Invent a letter of bad news from home.
I hung my head and tried to look as though,
By keeping such a brave stiff upper lip
And just not blubbing, I was noble too.
I sought out Mandeville. "I say," I said,
"I'm frightfully sorry I can't fight today.
I've just received some rotten news from home:
My mater's very ill." No need for more –
His arm was round my shoulder comforting:
"All right, old chap. Of course I understand."

Before the hymn the Skipper would announce
The latest names of those who'd lost their lives
For King and Country and the Dragon School.

56

Sometimes his gruff old voice was full of tears
When a particular favourite had been killed.
Then we would hear the nickname of the boy,
'Pongo' or 'Podge', and how he'd played 3Q
For Oxford and, if only he had lived,
He might have played for England – which he did,
But in a grimmer game against the Hun.
And then we'd all look solemn, knowing well
There'd be no extra holiday today.

The Dragon School

And we were told we each must do our bit,
And so we knitted shapeless gloves from string
For men in mine-sweepers, and on the map
We stuck the Allied flags along the Somme;
Visited wounded soldiers; learned by heart
Those patriotic lines of Oxenham

> What can a little chap do
> For his country and for you –

"He can boil his head in the stew",
We added, for the trenches and the guns
Meant less to us than bicycles and gangs
And marzipan and what there was for prep.

Take me, my Centaur bike, down Linton Road,
Gliding by newly planted almond trees
Where the young dons with wives in tussore clad
Were building in the morning of their lives
Houses for future Dragons. Rest an arm
Upon the post of the allotment path,
Then dare the slope! We choked in our own dust,
The narrowness of the footpath made our speed
Seem swift as light. May-bush and elm flashed by,
Allotment holders turning round to stare,
Potatoes in their hands. Speed-wobble! Help!
And, with the Sturmey-Archer three-speed gear
Safely in bottom, resting from the race
We pedalled round the new-mown meadow-grass
By Marston Ferry with its punt and chain.

St Philip & St James.

Show me thy road, Crick, in the early spring:
Laurel and privet and laburnum ropes
And gabled-gothic houses gathered round
Thy mothering spire, St. Philip and St. James.
Here by the low brick semi-private walls
Bicycling past a trotting butcher's-cart,
I glimpsed, behind lace curtains, silver hair
Of sundry old Professors. Here were friends
Of Ruskin, Newman, Pattison and Froude
Among their books and plants and photographs
In comfortable twilight. But for me,

Less academic, red-brick Chalfont Road
Meant great-aunt Wilkins, tea and buttered toast.
    Ronald Hughes Wright, come with me once again
Bicycling off to churches in the town:
St. Andrew's first, with neo-Norman apse,
St. Old's – distinctly Evangelical –
And, Lower still, St. Ebbe's, which smelt of gas.
In New Inn Hall Street dare the double doors,
Partitions and red baize till stands revealed
Peter-le-Bailey's Irish gothic nave.
    St. Giles' had still a proper fair-ground air,

For Oxford once had been a Cotswold town
Standing in water meadows of the Thames:
The cattle moaned in pens on Gloucester Green;
In George Street there were country cottages;
And thy weak Dec., St. George-the-Martyr's church,
Prepared us for our final port of call –
St. Aloysius of the Church of Rome.
Its incense, reliquaries, brass and lights
Made all seem plain and trivial back at school.

One lucky afternoon in Chaundy's shop
I bought a book with tipped-in colour plates –
'City of Dreaming Spires' or some such name –
Soft late-Victorian water-colours framed
Against brown paper pages. Thus it was
'Sunset in Worcester Gardens' meant for me
Such beauty in that black and shallow pool
That even today, when from the ilex tree

St Barnabas.

"Dreaming Spires"

I see its shining length, I fail to hear
The all-too-near and omnipresent train.
The Founder's Tower in Magdalen still seems drowned
In red Virginia creeper, and The High
Has but one horse-tram down its famous length,
While a gowned Doctor of Divinity
Enters the porch of Univ.; Christ Church stairs
(A single column supporting the intricate roof),
Wallflowers upon the ruined city wall,
Wistaria-mantled buildings in St. John's –
All that was crumbling, picturesque and quaint
Informed my taste and sent me biking off,
Escaped from games, for Architecture bound.
    Can words express the unexampled thrill
I first enjoyed in Norm., E.E. and Dec.?
Norm., crude and round and strong and primitive,

E.E., so lofty, pointed, fine and pure,
And Dec. the high perfection of it all,
Flowingly curvilinear, from which
The Perp. showed such a 'lamentable decline'.
Who knew what undiscovered glories hung
Waiting in locked-up churches – vaulting shafts,
Pillar-piscinas, floreated caps.,
Squints, squinches, low side windows, quoins and groins –
Till I had roused the Vicar, found the key,
And made a quick inspection of the church?
Then, full of my discovery returned,
Hot from my bicycle to Gerald Haynes.

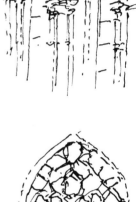

  Much do I owe this formidable man
(Harrow and Keble): from his shambling height
Over his spectacles he nodded down.
We called him 'Tortoise'. From his lower lip
Invariably hung a cigarette.
A gym-shoe in his hand, he stood about
Waiting for misdemeanours – then he'd pounce:
"Who's talking here?" The dormitory quailed.
"Who's talking?" Then, though innocent myself,
A schoolboy hero to the dorm at last,
Bravely I answered, "Please, sir, it was me."
"All right. Bend over." A resounding three
From the strong gym-shoe brought a gulp of pain.
"I liked the way you took that beating, John.
Reckon yourself henceforth a gentleman."
Were those the words that made me follow him,
Waiting for hours in churches while he fixed
His huge plate camera up and, a black cloth

Over his bald head, photographed the font?
Was that the reason why the pale grey slides
Of tympana, scratch dials and Norfolk screens
So pleased me at his lectures? I think not:
Rather his kindness and his power to share
Joys of his own, churches and botany,
With those of us whose tastes he could inform.
He motor-bicycled his life away,
Looking for orchids in the Wytham Woods,
And Early English in Northamptonshire.
He was the giver: ours it was to take.

    The bindweed hung in leafy loops
        O'er half a hundred hawthorn caves,
    For Godstow bound, the white road wound
        In swirls of dust and narrow shaves,
    And we were biking, Red Sea troops,
        Between the high cow-parsley waves.

    Port Meadow's level green grew near
        With Wytham Woods and Cumnor Hurst:
    I clicked my Sturmey-Archer gear
        And pedalled till I nearly burst –
    And, king of speed, attained the lead
        And got to gushing Godstow first.

    The skiffs were moored above the lock,
        They bumped each other side to side:
    I boarded one and made her rock –
        "Shut up, you fool," a master cried.
    By reed and rush and alder-bush
        See soon our long procession glide.

There is a world of water weed
    Seen only from a shallow boat:
Deep forests of the bladed reed
    Whose wolves are rats of slimy coat,
Whose yellow lily-blossoms need
    Broad leaves to keep themselves afloat.

A heaving world, half-land, half-flood;
    It rose and sank as ripples rolled,
The hideous larva from the mud
    Clung to a reed with patient hold,
Waiting to break its sheath and make
    An aeroplane of green and gold.

The picnic and the orchid hunt,
    On Oxey mead the rounders played,
The belly-floppers from the punt,
    The echoes that our shouting made:
The rowing back, relaxed and slack,
    The shipping oars in Godstow shade . . .

Once more we biked beside the hedge –
    And darker seemed the hawthorn caves
And lonelier looked the water's edge,
    And we were sad returning slaves
To bell and rule and smell of school,
    Beyond the high cow-parsley waves.

The Underground.

CHAPTER VI

LONDON ✎

The house in Chelsea ✎ Hannah Wallis
leaves ✎ new friends to bridge ✎ Ronnie
Wright and the author travel over whole
Underground system ✎ second-hand books
✎ steel engravings of Greek Revival
buildings ✎ thoughts and associations of
Sunday Evensong ✎

When I returned from school I found we'd moved:
    "53 Church Street. Yes, the slummy end" –
    A little laugh accompanied the joke,
For we were Chelsea now and we had friends
Whose friends had friends who knew Augustus John:
We liked bold colour schemes – orange and black –
And clever daring plays about divorce
At the St. Martin's. Oh, our lives were changed!
Ladies with pearls and hyphenated names
Supplanted simpler aunts from Muswell Hill:
A brand-new car and brand-new chauffeur came
To carry off my father to the Works.
                        Old Hannah Wallis left:
For years she'd listened to me reading verse;
Tons, if you added them, of buttered toast
Had she and I consumed through all the days
In happy Highgate. Now her dear old face,

Black bonnet, sniffs and comfortable self
Were gone to Tottenham where her daughter lived.
　　　What is it first breeds insecurity?
Perhaps a change of house? I missed the climb
By garden walls and fences where a stick,
Dragged on the palings, clattered to my steps.
I missed the smell of trodden leaves and grass,
Millfield and Merton Lanes and sheep-worn tracks
Under the hawthorns west of Highgate ponds.
I missed the trams, the few North London trains,
The frequent Underground to Kentish Town.
Here in a district only served by bus,
Here on an urban level by the Thames –
I never really liked the Chelsea house.
"It's simply sweet, Bess," visitors exclaimed,
Depositing their wraps and settling down
To a nice rubber. "So artistic, too."
To me the house was poky, dark and cramped,
Haunted by quarrels and the ground-floor ghost.
I'd slam behind me our green garden door –
Well do I recollect that bounding thrill! –
And hare to Cheyne Gardens – free! free! free! –
By Lawrence Street and Upper Cheyne Row,
Safe to the tall red house of Ronnie Wright.
　　　Great was my joy with London at my feet –
All London mine, five shillings in my hand
And not expected back till after tea!
Great was our joy, Ronald Hughes Wright's and mine,
To travel by the Underground all day
Between the rush hours, so that very soon

There was no station, north to Finsbury Park,
To Barking eastwards, Clapham Common south,
No temporary platform in the west
Among the Actons and the Ealings, where
We had not once alighted. Metroland
Beckoned us out to lanes in beechy Bucks –
Goldschmidt and Howland (in a wooden hut
Beside the station): 'Most attractive sites
Ripe for development'; Charrington's for coal;
And not far off the neo-Tudor shops.
We knew the different railways by their smells.
The City and South reeked like a changing-room;
Its orange engines and old rolling-stock,
Its narrow platforms, undulating tracks,
Seemed even then historic. Next in age,
The Central London, with its cut-glass shades
On draughty stations, had an ozone smell –
Not seaweed-scented ozone from the sea
But something chemical from Birmingham.
When, in a pause between the stations, quiet
Descended on the carriage we would talk
Loud gibberish in angry argument,
Pretending to be foreign.
                                    Then I found
Second-hand bookshops in the Essex Road,
Stacked high with powdery leather flaked and dry,
Gilt letters on red labels – *Mason's Works*
(But volume II is missing), Young's *Night Thoughts*,
Falconer's *Shipwreck* and *The Grave* by Blair,
A row of Scott, for certain incomplete,

And always somewhere Barber's *Isle of Wight*;
The antiquarian works that no one reads –
Church Bells of Nottingham, *Baptismal Fonts*
('Scarce, 2s. 6d., a few plates slightly foxed').
Once on a stall in Farringdon Road I found
An atlas folio of great lithographs,
View of Ionian Isles, flyleaf inscribed
By Edward Lear – and bought it for a bob.

Bookstalls – Farringdon Rd.

Perhaps one day I'll find a 'first' of Keats,
Wedged between Goldsmith and *The Law of Torts*;
Perhaps – but that was not the reason why
Untidy bookshops gave me such delight.
It was the smell of books, the plates in them,
Tooled leather, marbled paper, gilded edge,
The armorial book-plate of some country squire,
From whose tall library windows spread his park

On which this polished spine may once have looked,
From whose twin candlesticks may once have shone
Soft beams upon the spacious title-page.
Forgotten poets, parsons with a taste
For picturesque descriptions of a hill
Or ruin in the parish, pleased me much;
But steel engravings pleased me most of all –
Volumes of London views or Liverpool,
Or Edinburgh, 'The Athens of the North'.
I read the prose descriptions, gazed and gazed
Deep in the plates, and heard again the roll
Of market-carts on cobbles, coach-doors slammed
Outside the posting inn; with couples walked
Toward the pillared entrance of the church
'Lately erected from designs by Smirke';
And sauntered in some newly planted square.
Outside the bookshop, treasure in my hands,
I scarcely saw the trams or heard the bus
Or noticed modern London: I was back
With George the Fourth, post-horns, street-cries and bells.
"More books," my mother sighed as I returned;
My father, handing to me half-a-crown,
Said, "If you must buy books, then buy the best."
    All silvery on frosty Sunday nights
Were City steeples white against the stars.
And narrowly the chasms wound between
Italianate counting-houses, Roman banks,
To this church and to that. Huge office-doors,
Their granite thresholds worn by weekday feet
(Now far away in slippered ease at Penge),

St Botolph – Aldersgate.

Stood locked. St. Botolph this, St. Mary that
Alone shone out resplendent in the dark.
I used to stand by intersecting lanes
Among the silent offices, and wait,
Choosing which bell to follow: not a peal,
For that meant somewhere active; not St. Paul's,
For that was too well-known. I liked things dim –
Some lazy Rector living in Bexhill
Who most unwillingly on Sunday came
To take the statutory services.
A single bell would tinkle down a lane:
My echoing steps would track the source of sound –
A cassocked verger, bell-rope in his hands,
Called me to high box pews, to cedar wood

St Mary Aldermanbury.

(Like incense where no incense ever burned),
To ticking gallery-clock, and charity bench,
And free seats for the poor, and altar-piece –
Gilded Commandment boards – and sword-rests made
For long-discarded aldermanic pomp.
A hidden organist sent reedy notes
To flute around the plasterwork. I stood,
And from the sea of pews a single head
With cherries nodding on a black straw hat
Rose in a neighbouring pew. The caretaker?
Or the sole resident parishioner?
And so once more, as for three hundred years,
This carven wood, these grey memorial'd walls
Heard once again the Book of Common Prayer,
While somewhere at the back the verger, now
Turned Parish Clerk, would rumble out "Amen."
'Twas not, I think, a conscious search for God
That brought me to these dim forgotten fanes.
Largely it was a longing for the past,
With a slight sense of something unfulfilled;
And yet another feeling drew me there,
A sense of guilt increasing with the years –
"When I am dead you will be sorry, John" –
Here I could pray my mother would not die.
Thus were my London Sundays incomplete
If unaccompanied by Evening Prayer.
How trivial used to seem the Underground,
How worldly looked the over-lighted west,
How different and smug and wise I felt
When from the east I made my journey home!

Entrance Gates
Marlborough

CHAPTER VII
MARLBOROUGH ✒

Lucretian pleasure in a hot bath ✒ arriving
as a new boy ✒ sense of impending doom ✒
rules ✒ immunity during Chapel services ✒
Upper School ✒ its ranks ✒ evening prep
✒ scavenging ✒ beatings after prep ✒ 'Big
Fire' ✒ inexplicable desires ✒ attempt to
explain them ✒ going 'down town' with a
motor-car enthusiast ✒ bicycling to
Hackpen with him ✒ increased delight in
water-colours, architecture and literature ✒
ecstasy ✒

Luxuriating backwards in the bath,
   I swish the warmer water round my legs
     Towards my shoulders, and the waves of heat
Bring those five years of Marlborough through to me,
In comfortable retrospect: 'Thank God
I'll never have to go through them again.'
As with my toes I reach towards the tap
And turn it to a trickle, stealing warm
About my tender person, comes a voice,
An inner voice that calls, 'Be fair! be fair!
It was not quite as awful as you think.'
In steam like this the changing-room was bathed;
Pink bodies splashed hot water on themselves
After the wonderful release from games,
When Atherton would lead the songs we sang.

I see the tall Memorial Reading Room,
Which smelt of boots and socks and water-pipes,
Its deaf invigilator on his throne –
"Do you tickle your arse with a feather, Mr. Purdick?"
"What?"
"Particularly nasty weather, Mr. Purdick!"
"Oh."

And, as the water cools, the Marlborough terms
Form into seasons Winter starts us off,
Lasting two years, for we were new boys twice –
Once in a junior, then a senior house.
Spring has its love and summer has its art:
It is the winter that remains with me,
Black as our college suits, as cold and thin.

Doom! Shivering doom! Clutching a leather grip
Containing things for the first night of term –
House-slippers, sponge-bag, pyjams, Common Prayer,
My health certificate, photographs of home
(Where were my bike, my playbox and my trunk?) –
I walked with strangers down the hill to school.
The town's first gaslights twinkled in the cold.
Deserted by the coaches, poorly served
By railway, Marlborough was a lonely place;
The old Bath Road, in chalky whiteness, raised
Occasional clouds of dust as motors passed.

Those few who read Dean Farrar's *Eric* now
Read merely for a laugh; yet still for me
That mawkish and oh-so-melodious book
Holds one great truth – through every page there runs
The schoolboy sense of an impending doom

C House
Marlborough

Which goes with rows of desks and clanging bells.
It filters down from God, to Master's Lodge,
Through housemasters and prefects to the fags
    Doom! Shivering doom! Inexorable bells
To early school, to chapel, school again:

Compulsory constipation, hurried meals
Bulked out with Whipped Cream Walnuts from the town.
At first there was the dread of breaking rules –
"Betjeman, you know that new boys mustn't show
Their hair below the peak of college caps:
Stand still and have your face slapped." "Sorry, Jones."
The dread of beatings! Dread of being late!

Chapel Door.

And, greatest dread of all, the dread of games!
    "The centre and the mainspring of your lives,
The inspiration for your work and sport,
The corporate life of this great public school
Spring from its glorious chapel. Day by day
You come to worship in its noble walls,
Hallowed by half a century of prayer."
The Old Marlburian bishop thundered on
When all I worshipped were the athletes, ranged
In the pews opposite. "Be pure," he cried,
And, for a moment, stilled the sea of coughs.
"Do nothing that would make your mother blush
If she could see you. When the Tempter comes
Spurn him and God will lift you from the mire."
Oh, who is God? O tell me, who is God?
Perhaps He hides behind the reredos . . .
Give me a God whom I can touch and see.
The bishop was more right than he could know,
For safe in G. F. Bodley's greens and browns,
Safe in the surge of undogmatic hymns,
The Chapel *was* the centre of my life –
The only place where I could be alone.

    There was a building known as Upper School
(Abolished now, thank God, and all its ways),
An eighteen-fifty warehouse smelling strong
Of bat-oil, biscuits, sweat and rotten fruit.
The corporate life of which the bishop spoke,
At any rate among the junior boys,
Went on within its echoing whitewashed walls.
    Great were the ranks and privileges there:

Four captains ruled, selected for their brawn
And skill at games; and how we reverenced them!
Twelve friends they chose as brawny as themselves.
'Big Fire' we called them; lording it they sat
In huge armchairs beside the warming flames
Or played at indoor hockey in the space
Reserved for them. The rest of us would sit
Crowded on benches round another grate.

    Before the master came for evening prep
The captains entered at official pace
And, walking down the alley-way of desks,
Beat on their level lids with supple canes.
This was the sign for new boys to arise,
To pick up paper, apple-cores and darts
And fill huge baskets with the muck they found;
Then, wiping hands upon grey handkerchiefs
And trousers, settle down to Latin prose.

    Upper School captains had the power to beat:
Maximum six strokes, usually three.
My frequent crime was far too many books,
So that my desk lid would not shut at all:
"Come to Big Fire then, Betjeman, after prep."
I tried to concentrate on delicate points –
Ut, whether final or consecutive?
(Oh happy private-school days when I knew!) –
While all the time I thought of pain to come.
Swift after prep all raced towards 'Big Fire',
Giving the captain space to swing his cane:
"*One*," they would shout and downward came the blow;
"*Two*" (rather louder); then, exultant, "*Three*!"

And some in ecstasy would bellow *"Four."*
These casual beatings brought us no disgrace,
Rather a kind of glory. In the dorm,
Comparing bruises, other boys could show
Far worse ones that the beaks and prefects made.

    No, Upper School's most terrible disgrace
Involved a very different sort of pain.
Our discontents and enmities arose
Somewhere about the seventh week of term:
The holidays too far off to count the days
Till our release, the weeks behind, a blank.
"Haven't you heard?" said D. C. Wilkinson.
"Angus is to be basketed tonight."
Why Angus . . .? Never mind. The victim's found.
Perhaps he sported coloured socks too soon,
Perhaps he smarmed his hair with scented oil,
Perhaps he was 'immoral' or a thief.
We did not mind the cause: for Angus now
The game was up. His friends deserted him,
And after his disgrace they'd stay away
For fear of being basketed themselves.
"*By* the boys, *for* the boys. The boys know best.
Leave it to them to pick the rotters out
With that rough justice decent schoolboys know."
And at the end of term the victim left –
Never to wear an old Marlburian tie.

    In quieter tones we asked in Hall that night
Neighbours to pass the marge; the piles of bread
Lay in uneaten slices with the jam.
Too thrilled to eat we raced across the court

Under the frosty stars to Upper School.
Elaborately easy at his desk
Sat Angus, glancing through *The Autocar*.
Fellows walked past him trying to make it look
As if they didn't know his coming fate,
Though the boy's body called "Unclean! Unclean!"
And all of us felt goody-goody-good,
Nice wholesome boys who never sinned at all.
At ten to seven 'Big Fire' came marching in
Unsmiling, while the captains stayed outside
(For this was 'unofficial'). Twelve to one:
What chance had Angus? They surrounded him,
Pulled off his coat and trousers, socks and shoes
And, wretched in his shirt, they hoisted him
Into the huge waste-paper basket; then
Poured ink and treacle on his head. With ropes
They strung the basket up among the beams,
And as he soared I only saw his eyes
Look through the slats at us who watched below.
Seven. "It's prep". They let the basket down
And Angus struggled out. "Left! Right! Left! Right!"
We stamped and called as, stained and pale, he strode
Down the long alley-way between the desks,
Holding his trousers, coat and pointed shoes.
"You're for it next," said H. J. Anderson.
"I'm not." "You are. I've heard." So all that term
And three terms afterwards I crept about,
Avoiding public gaze. I kept my books
Down in the basement where the boot-hole was
And by its fishtail gas-jet nursed my fear.

The smell of trodden leaves beside the Kennet,
    On Sunday walks, with Swinburne in my brain,
November showers upon the chalk dust, when it
    Would turn to streaming milk in Manton Lane
And coming back to feel one's footsteps drag
At smells of burning toast and cries of "Fag!".

The after-light that hangs along the hedges,
    On sunward sides of them when sun is down,
The sprinkled lights about the borough's edges,
    The pale green gas-lamps winking in the town,
The waiting elm-boughs black against the blue
Which still to westward held a silver hue –

Alone beside the fives-courts pacing, pacing,
    Waiting for God knows what. O stars above!
My clothes clung tight to me, my heart was racing:
    Perhaps what I was waiting for was love!
And what is love? And wherefore is its shape
To do with legs and arms and waist and nape?

First tremulous desires in Autumn stillness –
    Grey eyes, lips laughing at another's joke,
A nose, a cowlick – a delightful illness
    That put me off my food and off my stroke.
Here, 'twixt the church tower and the chapel spire
Rang sad and deep the bells of my desire.

Desire for what? I think I can explain.
The boys I worshipped did not notice me:
The boys who noticed me I did not like . . .
And life was easier in terms of jokes
And gossip, chattered with contemporaries –
And then there came my final summer term.

Marlborough High St.

"Coming down town?" I had not thought of him,
Though for four years we'd struggled up the school
In the same house. He was a noisy boy,
One of a gang so mad on motor-cars
That I, the aesthete, hardly noticed him.
Why should he want to go down town with me?

Perhaps because his friends had parents down,
Perhaps because we both were on our own –
But off we walked to Stratton, Sons & Mead
Down the hot High Street. "Can't think why we pay
Threepence at Knapton's for a water ice
When Ducks' is tuppence. There's a Frazer-Nash.
Gosh, what an engine! Did you hear her rev?"
Returning with sardines and sausages,
We found the College empty – free till six –
All Wiltshire winking in the summer sun.

      We changed and bicycled to Silbury
By burnt-up hawthorn edged again with white
From chalk dust whirled by Fords and Lancias
Scorching to Bath. Up Seven Barrows Hill
We overtook a six-ton Sentinel,
Our bike chains creaking with the strain. The heat
Cooled into green below the waiting elms
That rampart round sepulchral Avebury.
And gliding through the Winterbournes was peace:
Calm as canoeing were those winding lanes
Of meadowsweet and umbelliferae.

      He took the lead and raced for Hackpen Hill,
Up, up and up and waited at the top.
He sat among the harebells in his shorts,
Hugging his knees till I caught up with him.
A lock of hair kept falling on his face;
He pushed it back and, looking past me, said:
"Why do you always go about with Black?"
"I haven't thought. I'm used to him, you know."
"I never liked the fellow." Here was love

Too deep for words or touch. The golden downs
Looked over elm tops islanded in mist,
And short grass twinkled with blue butterflies.
Henceforward Marlborough shone.

                                I used to sketch
Under the tutelage of Mr. Hughes,
Who taught us art and let us speak our minds –
And now how lovely seemed the light and shade
On cob and thatch of Wiltshire cottages.

When trout waved lazy in the clear chalk streams,
Glory was in me as I tried to paint
The stretch of meadow and the line of downs,
Putting in buttercups in bright gamboge,
Ultramarine and cobalt for the sky,
With blotting-paper, while the page was wet,
For cloud effects. The eighteenth-century front
Of Ramsbury Manor, solid on its slope,
With subtly curving drive towards the lake,

Calm and trout-plopping in surrounding trees,
Defied my brush. What matter? – poetry
Poured from my pen to keep the ecstasy.
Those were the days when Huxley's *Antic Hay*
Shocked our conventions, when from month to month
I rushed to buy *The London Mercury*,
And moved from Austin Dobson on to Pope.

What joy abounded when the shadows raced
From Rockley to Old Eagle over grass
Faster than I could run! I was released
Into Swinburnian stanzas with the wind.
I felt so strong that I could leap a brook,
So clever, I could master anything;
For Marlborough now was home and beautiful.
Then on the final morning of the term,
Wearing his going-away suit, which had lain
Pressed by his mattress all the previous night,
He came and handed me an envelope
And went without a word. Inside I found
The usual smiling farewell photograph.

Ramsbury Manor.

CHAPTER VIII

CORNWALL IN ADOLESCENCE ✒

Thoughts of the author's father as he is
driven to Cornwall ✒ the author's mother ✒
her sunshine reverie ✒ father's arrival ✒
a row at breakfast ✒ bicycling to St. Ervan
✒ its lonely rector ✒ his talk ✒ lends Arthur
Machen's 'The Secret Glory' ✒ author's
fruitless quest of mystical experience ✒
self-conscious superiority ✒ Aunt Elsie ✒
love for Biddy Walsham ✒

The Arrol-Johnston spun him down to Slough –
Cornwall the object of the early start
And Newbury a foretaste of the goal,
With Trust House lunch and double Scotch at two.
The golf bag shifted as she took the hill
And set a-swing a dangling metal case
That held a piece of sponge for cleaning balls –
A dozen Silver Kings with bramble marks
To sail the fairway, chip upon the green,
And tittup straight and true into the hole.
A smell of leather and of Harris tweed;
The gun-case in the back: Okehampton-wards,
Through broad red Devon: there's a field of roots,
A covey and an orchard and a farm.
"It's getting dark, Bates, switch the headlights on."

Here, in his deafness and his loneliness,
My father's sad grey eyes in gathering dusk
Saw Roughtor and Brown Willy hide the view
Of that bold coast-line where he was not born –
Not born but would he had been, would he had
More right than just the price of them to wear
Those tweeds and leather leggings! "Hurry, Bates."
'His Gibson Girl, his white, his good queen Bess
Straw-hatted bicycling down Surrey lanes . . .
Her welcome for him coming home from work . . .
That early flat, electrically lit,
Red silk and leather in the dining-room,
Beads round the drawing-room electrolier . . .
Singing in bed, to make the youngster laugh,
Tosti's "Goodbye", Lord Henry's "Echo Song" –
And windy walks on Sunday to the Heath,
While dogs were barking round the White Stone pond . . .'

These were the years when love gave way to fear.
I feared my father, loved my mother more,
And just because of this would criticize,
In my own mind, the artless things she said.
        "Dr. Macmillan, who's so good and cheap,
Says I will tire my kidneys if I stoop,
And oh, I *do* love gardening, for now
My garden is the last thing I have left.
You'll help me with the weeding, won't you, John?
He says my teeth are what is wrong, the roots
Have been attacked by dangerous bacilli
Which breed impurities through all my blood,
And this inflames my kidneys. Mrs. Bent
Had just the same (but not, of course, so bad);
She nearly died, poor thing, till Captain Bent
Insisted she should have them out at once.
But mine are ossified into my gums –
No dentist could extract them. Listen, John . . ."
Poor mother, walking bravely on the lawn,
Her body one huge toothache! Would she die?
And if she died could I forgive myself?
"Besides there's what we pay in bills for you.
We've sent you to a most expensive school,
And John, oh John, you've disappointed us.
Your father said to me the other day
How much he wished you were like other boys.
He says that you should earn your keep by now,
By working at the bench. I did my best
To make him give you just another chance."
        Her wit, her gaiety, the jokes we shared,

The love for her that waited underneath,
I kept in check; and as the motor sped
At thirty-five through Shepton on to Wells
Bearing its chauffeur-driven bogey-man,
Down here in Cornwall I would run away
And leave her as we let the tension mount
Through all the Cornish summer afternoon;
     "See how the wind has knocked the rambler down
And damaged my gloxinias. Thank you, Maud.
And now if you will find my spectacles,
And put the ashtray there. That's better. Ah . . .
'Peace, perfect peace.' My pain is nearly gone.
Yes, thank you, Maud. Is everything prepared?
He should be here by dinner. Keep it hot.
Put the potatoes on to boil in time:
You know he's very angry if they're hard.
And put some water in his dressing-room –
The white enamel jug below the stairs –
You know he's very angry if there's none.
And put the drinks out on the silver tray,
And see the whiskey is decanted, Maud:
You know he's very angry if it's not.
And let me know when Master John is back.
Oh, what it is to run a country house!
Certainly not a holiday for me.
The constant worry simply knocks me up;
Our dear old Doctor Blaber used to say,
'Bessie, I fear, is rather delicate.'
What would he say, then, if he saw me now –
Twenty-five years without a holiday,

Housekeeping for a husband and a son?
Five-thirty! Two more hours of quiet bliss!
From this verandah I can see the world
And be at one with Nature. Think Good Thoughts,
And merge myself into the Infinite.
There's Ethel Harden coming up the lane,
I expect she's been to Padstow . . . Oh, how kind!
She promised she would bring me back some wool.
If only John were kind to me like that . . .
Who are those vulgar people on the links –
So out of touch with all the beauty here?
If only Ernest were more sensitive . . .

But never mind. Think Good Thoughts, Bess, cheer up,
And saturate your soul with loveliness.
Knowledge is Power – breathe deeply – Power is Life,
God is the Source of Infinite Resolve,
Ill-health is Evil, therefore Health is God.
I'll think of all the nice things in the world:
A cup of tea, a sunny afternoon,
A snooze, a cigarette, this comfy chair,
A book, *The Education of Eric Lane* –
Now that reminds me. Coo-ee! Jonathan!
Maud! Can you come a moment? Maud! . . . Ah, Maud,
I cannot move, I am too comfortable:
I really should have sent for Master John,
But he is out – my book – the sitting-room –
And – if you're not too busy – bring it here . . .
The one from Boots's with the marker in –
Stephen McKenna, such a clever man . . .
Not there? It must be in my bedroom then.
Ah! *Thank* you . . . If the kettle's on the boil,
Just fill this bottle for me once again.
Where was I? 'And when Cynthia saw his face,
So proudly sensitive, the easy way
He wore those old, albeit well-cut, tweeds
With all the breeding that was Eric Lane,
And saw the twinkle in his blue-grey eyes,
She knew, instinctively, she was forgiven.' "

    A motor broke the spell and that was that;
And here was home, and here the gate, and there
The Arrol-Johnston crawling down the lane.

    And on the morning after burst the storm:

"How often have I said the bacon's cold?
Confound it, Bess! Confound! When will they learn?"
Bang! Boom! His big fists set the cups a-dance,
The willow-pattern shivered on the shelves,
His coat-sleeve swept an ash-tray to the floor . . .
"Just down for breakfast, sir? You're good enough
To honour us by coming down at ten!
Don't fidget, boy. Attention when I speak!
As I was saying – now I look at you –
Bone-lazy, like my eldest brother Jack,
A rotten, low, deceitful little snob.
Yes, I'm in trade and proud of it, I am!"
Black waves of hate went racing round the room;
My gorge was stuck with undigested toast.
And did this woman once adore this man?
And did he love her for her form and face?
I drew my arm across my eyes to hide
The horror in them at the wicked thoughts.
"My boy, it's no good sulking. Listen here.
You'll go to Bates and order me the car,
You'll caddy for me on the morning round,
This afternoon you'll help me dig for bait,
You'll weed the lawn and, when you've finished that,
I'll find another job for you to do.
I'll keep you at it as I've kept myself –
I'll have obedience! Yes, by God, I will!"
"You damn well won't! I'm going out to-day!"
I darted for the door. My father rose.
My saintly mother, on her serious face
A regal look of dignified reproach –

St Levan

"They both are in the wrong" – now seized her chance:
She waved an arm and dropped her cigarette.
"Come back!" she cried, and heard her cry ring out
As rang the martyred wife's or mother's cry
In many a Temple Thurston she had read,
Or Philip Gibbs: "He *is* your father, John!"
I scraped my wrist along the unstained oak
And slammed the door against my father's weight –
And ran like mad and ran like mad and ran . . .
"I'm free! I'm free!" The open air was warm
And heavy with the scent of flowering mint,
And beetles waved on bending leagues of grass,
And all the baking countryside was kind.

Dear lanes of Cornwall! With a one-inch map,
A bicycle and well-worn *Little Guide*,
Those were the years I used to ride for miles
To far-off churches. One of them that year
So worked on me that, if my life was changed,
I owe it to St. Ervan and his priest
In their small hollow deep in sycamores.

St Ervan.

The time was tea-time, calm free-wheeling time,
When from slashed tree-tops in the combe below
I heard a bell-note floating to the sun;
It gave significance to lichened stone
And large red admirals with outspread wings
Basking on buddleia. So, coasting down
In the cool shade of interlacing boughs,
I found St. Ervan's partly ruined church.
Its bearded Rector, holding in one hand
A gong-stick, in the other hand a book,
Struck, while he read, a heavy-sounding bell,
Hung from an elm bough by the churchyard gate.
"Better come in. It's time for Evensong."

　　There wasn't much to see, there wasn't much
The *Little Guide* could say about the church.
Holy and small and heavily restored,
It held me for the length of Evensong,
Said rapidly among discoloured walls,
Impatient of my diffident response.
"Better come in and have a cup of tea."
The Rectory was large, uncarpeted;
Books and oil-lamps and papers were about;
The study's pale green walls were mapped with damp;
The pitch-pine doors and window-frames were cracked;
Loose noisy tiles along the passages
Led to a waste of barely furnished rooms:
Clearly the Rector lived here all alone.

　　He talked of poetry and Cornish saints;
He kept an apiary and a cow;
He asked me which church service I liked best –

I told him Evensong . . . "And I suppose
You think religion's mostly singing hymns
And feeling warm and comfortable inside?"
And he was right: most certainly I did.
"Borrow this book and come to tea again."
With Arthur Machen's *Secret Glory* stuffed
Into my blazer pocket, up the hill
On to St. Merryn, down to Padstow Quay
In time for the last ferry back to Rock,
I bicycled – and found Trebetherick
A worldly contrast with my afternoon.

Padstow Quay.

I would not care to read that book again.
It so exactly mingled with the mood
Of those impressionable years, that now
I might be disillusioned. There were laughs
At public schools, at chapel services,
At masters who were still 'big boys at heart' –
While all the time the author's hero knew

FERRY

Padstow Ferry.

St Enodoc.

A Secret Glory in the hills of Wales:
Caverns of light revealed the Holy Grail
Exhaling gold upon the mountain-tops;
At "Holy! Holy! Holy!" in the Mass
King Brychan's sainted children crowded round,
And past and present were enwrapped in one.
　　　In quest of mystical experience
I knelt in darkness at St. Enodoc;
I visited our local Holy Well,
Whereto the native Cornish still resort
For cures for whooping-cough, and drop bent pins
Into its peaty water . . . Not a sign:

No mystical experience was vouchsafed:
The maidenhair just trembled in the wind
And everything looked as it always looked . . .
But somewhere, somewhere underneath the dunes,
Somewhere among the cairns or in the caves
The Celtic saints would come to me, the ledge
Of time we walk on, like a thin cliff-path
High in the mist, would show the precipice.

An only child, deliciously apart,
Misunderstood and not like other boys,
Deep, dark and pitiful I saw myself
In my mind's mirror, every step I took
A fascinating study to the world.
Box-wallahs, doctors, schoolmasters and dons,
The other parents of the holidays,
Seemed easier to deal with than my own.
In bungalows, with relics of the East
Spared from their London houses, they reclined
On sofas and with happy faces watched
Their bouncing young ones in the drawing-room
Roll up the carpet ready for a dance.
The jingle tinkled in the entrance-hall,
Japanese lanterns lit the sandy paths;
Over the tamarisks the summer night
Heard Melville Gideon on the gramophone.
        And one there was of all the adults there
Who took me at my reckoning of myself –
Aunt Elsie, aunt of normal Scottish boys,
Adopted aunt of lone abnormal me:
She understood us all, she treated us
With reason, waiting while we choked with rage.
"Aunt Elsie, surely I could have the car?"
The eucalyptus shivered in the drive,
The stars were out above the garage roof,
Night-scented stock and white tobacco plant
Gave way to petrol scent and came again.
A rival, changing gear along the lane,
Alone disturbed the wide September night.

"Come in, John, and I'll tell you why you can't."
And there, among the water-colours, screens,
Thick carpets, Whistler books and porcelain,
There, in that more-than-summer residence,
She would explain that I was still a boy.
   'Was still a boy?' Then what, by God, was this –
This tender, humble, unrequited love
For Biddy Walsham? What the worshipping
That put me off my supper, fixed my hair
Thick with Anzora for the dance tonight?
The Talbot-Darracq, with its leather seats
And Biddy in beside me! I could show
Double-declutching to perfection now.
What though the Stokeses were a field away?
Biddy would scream with laughter as I'd charge
Up the steep corner of Coolgrena drive,

And slip from top to second, down to first,
And almost seem to ram the bungalow,
And swirl around the terraced plateau, brake –
Then switch the headlights off and we would wait
While the recovering engine ticked to quiet
In comfortable darkness. If my hand
By accident should touch her hand, perhaps
The love in me would race along to her
On the electron principle, perhaps . . .?
"So surely, John, it's sensible to walk?"

Garden Trees Cornwall

H.C.

CHAPTER IX

THE OPENING WORLD ✎

Rooms of one's own at Magdalen ✎ The
George Restaurant, Oxford ✎ chatter of its
customers ✎ Sunday morning ✎ High Mass
at Pusey House ✎ sherry in Beaumont
Street with Colonel Kolkhorst ✎ songs sung
there ✎ introduction to country house life ✎
John Dugdale and his father and mother ✎
evening in the Cotswolds ✎ dinner in
Wadham with Maurice Bowra ✎ irregular
ode to Oxford ✎ 'Homage to Beethoven' ✎
the leisured set in Canterbury Quad ✎
Edward James ✎ author fails in Holy
Scripture ✎ becomes a private schoolmaster ✎

Balkan Sobranies in a wooden box,
The college arms upon the lid; Tokay
And sherry in the cupboard; on the shelves
The University Statutes bound in blue,
Crome Yellow, *Prancing Nigger*, Blunden, Keats.
My walls were painted Bursar's apple-green;
My wide-sashed windows looked across the grass
To tower and hall and lines of pinnacles.
The wind among the elms, the echoing stairs,
The quarters, chimed across the quiet quad
From Magdalen tower and neighbouring turret-clocks,
Gave eighteenth-century splendour to my state.

Magdalen Tower.

114

Privacy after years of public school;
Dignity after years of none at all –
First college rooms, a kingdom of my own:
What words of mine can tell my gratitude?
        No wonder, looking back, I never worked.
Too pleased with life, swept in the social round,
I soon left Old Marlburians behind.
(As one more solemn of our number said:
"Spiritually I was at Eton, John.")
I cut tutorials with wild excuse,
For life was luncheons, luncheons all the way –
And evenings dining with the Georgeoisie.
Open, swing doors, upon the lighted 'George'
And whiff of *vol-au-vent*! Behold the band
Sawing away at gems from *Chu Chin Chow*,
As Harold Acton and the punkahs wave:
"My dears, I want to rush into the fields
And slap raw meat with lilies."
But as the laughs grew long and loud I heard
The more insistent inner voice of guilt:
"Stop!" cried my mother from her bed of pain.
I heard my father in his factory say:
"Fourth generation, John, they look to you."
        "Harry Strathspey is coming if he can
After he's dined at Blenheim. Hamish says
That Ben has got twelve dozen Bollinger."
"And Sandy's going as a matelot."
"I will not have that Mr. Mackworth Price;
Graham will be so furious if he's asked –
We do *not* want another ghastly brawl " . . .

"Well, don't ask Graham, then." "I simply must."
"The hearties say they're going to break it up."
"Oh no, they're not. I've settled *them* all right,
I've bribed the Boat Club with a cask of beer."
Moon after parties: moon on Magdalen Tower,
And shadow on the place for climbing in . . .
Noise, then the great, deep silences again.

      Silk-dressing-gowned, to Sunday-morning bells,
Long after breakfast had been cleared in Hall,
I wandered to my lavender-scented bath;
Then, with a loosely knotted shantung tie
And hair well soaked in Delhez' Genêt d'Or,
Strolled to the Eastgate. Oxford marmalade
And a thin volume by Lowes Dickinson
But half-engaged my thoughts till Sunday calm
Led me by crumbling walls and echoing lanes,
Past college chapels with their organ-groan
And churches stacked with bicycles outside,
To worship at High Mass in Pusey House.

      Those were the days when that divine baroque
Transformed our English altars and our ways.
Fiddle-back chasuble in mid-Lent pink
Scandalized Rome and Protestants alike:
"Why do you try to ape the Holy See?"
"Why do you sojourn in a halfway house?"
And if these doubts had ever troubled me
(Praise God, they don't) I would have made the move.
What seemed to me a greater question then
Tugged and still tugs: Is Christ the Son of God?
Despite my frequent lapses into lust,

116

High Mass in Pusey House

117

Despite hypocrisy, revenge and hate,
I learned at Pusey House the Catholic faith.
Friends of those days, now patient parish priests,
By worldly standards you have not 'got on'
Who knelt with me as Oxford sunlight streamed
On some colonial bishop's broidered cope.
Some know for all their lives that Christ is God,
Some start upon that arduous love affair
In clouds of doubt and argument; and some
(My closest friends) seem not to want His love –
And why this is I wish to God I knew.
As at the Dragon School, so still for me
The steps to truth were made by sculptured stone,
Stained glass and vestments, holy-water stoups,
Incense and crossings of myself – the things
That hearty middle-stumpers most despise
As 'all the inessentials of the Faith'.

    What cranking-up of round-nosed Morrises
Among the bicycles of broad St. Giles'!
What mist of buds about the guardian elms
Before St. John's! What sense of joys to come
As opposite the Randolph's Gothic pile
We bought the Sunday newspapers and rush'd
Down Beaumont Street to Number 38
And Colonel Kolkhorst's Sunday-morning rout!

  D'ye ken Kolkhorst in his artful parlour,
  Handing out the drink at his Sunday morning gala?
  Some get sherry and some Marsala –
    With his arts and his crafts in the morning!

The over-crowded room was lit by gas
And smelt of mice and chicken soup and dogs.
Among the knick-knacks stood a photograph
Of that most precious Oxford essayist,
Upon whose margin Osbert Lancaster
Wrote 'Alma Pater' in his sloping hand.
George Alfred Kolkhorst, you whom nothing shocked,
Who never once betrayed a confidence,
No one believed you really were a don
Till Gerard Irvine (now a parish priest)
Went to your lecture on *Le Cid* and clapped.
You swept towards him, gowned, and turned him out.
I see the lines of laughter in your face,
I see you pouring sherry – round your neck
A lump of sugar hanging on a thread
'To sweeten conversation': to your ear
A trumpet held 'for catching good remarks.'
An earlier generation called you 'G'ug':
We called you 'Colonel' just because you were,
Though tall, so little like one. Round your room
The rhyming folklore grew luxuriant:

G'uggery G'uggery Nunc,
Your room is all cluttered with junk:
Candles, bamboonery,
Plush and saloonery –
Please pack it up in a trunk.*

* Words by Rev. Colin Gill, Rector of St. Magnus-the-Martyr, City of
London.

You loved the laughter at your own expense:

That's the wise G'ug, he says each thing twice over,
Lest you should think he never could recapture
That first fine *careful* rapture:*

How trivial and silly now they look
Set up in type, acknowledgments and all,
Those rhymes that rocked the room in Beaumont Street,
Preposterous as th' apostrophe in Gug,
Dear private giggles of a private world!
Alan Pryce-Jones came in a bathing-dress
And, seated at your low harmonium,
Struck up the Kolkhorst Sunday-morning hymn:
"There's a home for Colonel Kolkhorst" – final verse
ff with all the stops out:—

There Bignose plays the organ
    And the pansies all sing flat,
But G'ug's no ear for music,
    He never notices that.
The stairs are never smelly,
    The dogs are well-behaved
And the Colonel makes his *bons mots*
    To an audience of the saved.†

Perhaps you do. Perhaps you stand up there,
Waiting with sherry among other friends
Already come, till we rush up the stairs.

* Words by R. Browning and J. D. K. Lloyd, FSA.
† Words by A. Midlane (1825–1909), Osbert Lancaster and J. Betjeman.

Oxford May mornings! When the prunus bloomed
We'd drive to Sunday lunch at Sezincote:
First steps in learning how to be a guest,
First wood-smoke-scented luxury of life
In the large ambience of a country house.
Heavy with hawthorn scent were Cotswold lanes,
Golden the church towers standing in the sun,
And Gordon Russell with his arts and crafts,
Somewhere beyond in Broadway. Down the drive,
Under the early yellow leaves of oaks;
One lodge is Tudor, one in Indian style.
The bridge, the waterfall, the Temple Pool –
And there they burst on us, the onion domes,
Chajjahs and *chattris* made of amber stone:
'Home of the Oaks,' exotic Sezincote!
Stately and strange it stood, the Nabob's house,
Indian without and coolest Greek within,
Looking from Gloucestershire to Oxfordshire;
And, by supremest landscape-gardener's art,
The lake below the eastward slope of grass
Was made to seem a mighty river-reach
Curving along to Chipping Norton's hills.

    Crackle of gravel! in the entrance-hall
Boot-jacks and mattocks, hunting mackintosh,
And whips and sticks and barometric clock
Were Colonel Dugdale's; but a sheaf of bast
And gardening-basket told us of his wife.
"Camilla Russell – Bridget King-Tenison –
And Major Attlee – Patsy Rivington –
Shall we go in? I think it's rather late."

Dear Mrs. Dugdale, mother of us all,
In trailing and Edwardian-looking dress,
A Sargent portrait in your elegance,
Sweet confidante in every tale of woe!
She and her son and we were on the Left,
But Colonel Dugdale was Conservative.

From one end of the butler-tended board
The Colonel's eyes looked out towards the hills,
While at the other end our hostess heard
Political and undergraduate chat.
"Oh, Ethel," loudly Colonel Dugdale's voice
Boomed sudden down the table, "that manure –
I've had it shifted to the strawberry-beds."

"Yes, Arthur . . . Major Attlee, as you said,
Seventeen million of the poor Chinese
Eat less than half a calory a week?"

How proud beneath the swelling dome
I sang Lord Ullin's daughter
At Mrs. Dugdale's grand At Home
To Lady Horsbrugh-Porter.

So Sezincote became a second home.
The love between those seeming opposites,
Colonel and Mrs. Dugdale, warmed their guests.
The paddock where the Colonel's favourite mare,
His tried companion of the '14 war,
Grazed in retirement – what is in it now?
New owners wander to the Temple Pool
Where Mrs. Dugdale snipped exotic shrubs
With secateurs as on and on I talked.
The onion dome which listened all the time
To water filling after-tennis baths,
To water splashing over limestone rock
Under the primulas and thin bamboo,
The cottages and lanes and woods and paths
Are all so full of voices from the past
I do not dare return.
At six o'clock from Bourton-on-the-Hill
The bells rang out above the lump of oak;
A lighter peal from Longborough lingered on;
Moreton-in-Marsh came echoing from the vale . . .
So gently broke the triple waves of sound
On a still evening of enormous light

That, when they ceased, I almost seemed to hear
From open church-doors village voluntaries
A mile and more away.
                              It's time to go.
Dinner with Maurice Bowra sharp at eight –
High up in Wadham's hospitable quad:
The Gilbert Spencers and the Campbell Gray
Bright in the inner room; the brown and green
Of rows and rows of Greek and Latin texts;
The learning lightly worn; the grand contempt
For pedants, traitors and pretentiousness.
A dozen oysters and a dryish hock;
Claret and *tournedos*; a *bombe surprise* . . .
The fusillade of phrases ("I'm a man
More dined against than dining") rattled out
In that incisive voice and chucked away
To be re-used in envious common-rooms
By imitation Maurices. I learned,
If learn I could, how not to be a bore,
And merciless was his remark that touched
The tender spot if one were showing off.

Wadham College. Front Quad.

Within those rooms I met my friends for life.
True values there were handed on a plate
As easily as sprouts and aubergines:
"A very able man." "But what's he like?"
"I've told you. He's a very able man."

126

Magdalen College. New Buildings.

Administrators, professorial chairs
In subjects such as Civics, and the cad
Out for himself, pretending to be kind –
He summed them up in scathing epigram,
Occasionally shouting out the truth

In forceful nineteen-fourteen army slang;
And as the evening mellowed into port,
He read us poems. There I learned to love
That lord of landscape, Alfred Tennyson;
There first heard Thomas Hardy's poetry,
Master of metre, local as his lanes,
The one expressive village fatalist.
Yeats he would chant in deep sonórous voice;
Bring Rudyard Kipling – then so out-of-date –
To his full stature; show that wisdom was
Not memory-tests (as I had long supposed),
Not 'first-class brains' and swotting for exams,
But humble love for what we sought and knew.
King of a kingdom underneath the stars,
I wandered back to Magdalen, certain then,
As now, that Maurice Bowra's company
Taught me far more than all my tutors did.

Come, Michael Arthur Stratford Dugdale, rise,
     And Lionel Geoffrey Perry. It is ten.
Binsey to Cowley, Oxford open lies.
     They breakfasted at eight, the college men
In college blazers clad and college ties
     Who will be pouring out of lectures when
          Eleven strikes,
For morning coffee at 'The Super' bound,
     And stack their bikes
St. Mary Mag's Tractarian walls around.

          Rise! we ourselves are pledged to drink with Ben.
               John Edward Bowle
               Will bring his soul
And even Mr. Bryson may be coming.
Rise from your beds! The hawthorn trees are humming
With insects down the length of Banbury Road,
     The water splashes over Medley Weir.
     The freckled undergraduettes appear,
Handle-bar baskets heavy with the load
     Of books on Middle English. Up! Away!
We're lunching at the Liberal Club today
     Where, though the credit's good, the food is poor.
          And should a single Liberal dare
          To show his hunted features there
          We'll freeze him with a stony stare
     That drives him to the door.

New College calls us with her Wykehamists,
Old home of essays, gowns and lecture lists,
     Where Sparrow, with his cowlick lock of hair
          And schoolboy looks,
     Stands a young contrast to his antique books
On walls, floor, table, window-seats and chair.

What time magnolia's bursting into bloom
    By Balliol's brain-grey wall,
      See clever satyr sprawl
        And well-bred faun
Round 'Sligger' in his deck-chair on the lawn.
    Deep in their books they are, yet notice whom
They will, with cheerful shout across the grass
For peer and Isis Idol as they pass,
While Sandy Lindsay from his lodge looks down
    Dreaming of Adult Education where
      The pottery chimneys flare
On lost potential firsts in some less favoured town.

We'll thread the hurrying Corn and George Street crowds
    To the unlovely entrance of the OUDS
      And hear
How Harman Grisewood, in the tones which thrill
      His audience in *Lear*,
    Orders a postcard and a penny stamp;
While Emlyn Williams, palm to either ear,
    Struggles to learn a part,
And in the next-door room is heard the tramp
    And 'rhubarb, rhubarb' as the crowd rehearse
    A one-act play in verse,
Written by someone who is wedded still
    To Gordon Bottomley and Celtic Art.

And does an unimportant don
In Pembroke College linger on,
    With sported oak, alone?
Do nearby bells of low St. Ebbe's
    Ring all unnoticed there?
Can only climbing ivy see
That he for weeks has ceased to be,
While hungry spiders spin their webs
    Between his desk and chair,
Where he is sitting very still
With all Eternity to kill?
How empty, creeper-grown and odd
Seems lonely Pembroke's second quad!
    Still, when I see it, do I wonder why
    That college so polite and shy
Should have more character than Queen's
    Or Univ. splendid in The High.

The High.

Friends, we will let our final visit be
　　Oxford's epitome:
　　The place they call The House
　　That shelters A. L. Rowse,
Where the unnoticed canons and their wives
　　Live safe North Oxford lives
While peer and peasant tread the sculptured stair
　　The festal light to share
　　Of Christ Church hall.
Let the obscure cathedral's organ note
Out, out into the starry darkness float
O'er my friend Auden and the clever men,
Running like mad to miss the upper ten
Who burst from 'Peck' in Bullingdonian brawl,
　　Jostling some pale-faced victim, you or me.
　　I tell you, Brian Howard,
　　'Fore God, I am no coward –
But the triumphant Philistines I see,
And hear a helpless body splash in muddy Mercury.

Christchurch. Canterbury Quad.

With sports Bugattis roaring in my ears,
　　With 'Blackbirds' bursting from my gramophone,
Lunching with poets, dining late with peers,
　　I felt that I had come into my own.

What *was* my own? Large parts of it were jest.
　　Recall the music room in Holywell,
The nice North Oxford audience, velvet-dress'd,
　　Waiting a treat whose title promised well:

HOMAGE TO BEETHOVEN the posters show.
　　'Words: Thomas Driberg. Music: Archie Browne'.
Good wives of Heads of Houses, do you know
　　For what it is you've given your half-crown?

What was 'my own'? I partly liked to shock –
　　But strawberry-coloured trousers soon made way
For shirts by Hawes and Curtis, hats by Lock,
　　And suits for which my father had to pay.

What was my own? Week after sunny week
　　I climbed, still keeping in, I thought, with God,
Until I reached what seemed to me the peak –
　　The leisured set in Canterbury Quad.

The sun that shines on Edward James
　　Shines also down on me:
It's strange that two such simple names
　　Should spell such mystery.
The air he breathes, I breathe it too –
But where's he now? What does he do?

On tapestries from Brussels looms
　　The low late-'20s sunlight falls
In those black-ceilinged Oxford rooms

And on their silver-panelled walls;
ARS LONGA VITA BREVIS EST
Was painted round them – not in jest.

And who in those days thought it odd
    To liven breakfast with champagne
And watch, in Canterbury Quad,
    Pale undergraduates in the rain?
For, while we ate Virginia hams,
Contemporaries passed exams.

Tutorials and dons there were,
    And tests and teams and toughs and games –
But these were neither here nor there
    To such as me and Edward James:
We swung the incense-smoke about
To drive the smells of breakfast out,
And talked of Eliot and Wilde
    And Sachie's *Southern Baroque Art*,
While all the time our darling child,
    The poem we had learned by heart
(And wrote last night) must be recited,
Whether or not it were invited.

At William Morris how we laughed,
	And hairy tweeds and knitted ties:
Pub poets who from tankards quaff'd
	Glared up at us with angry eyes –
For, Regency before our time,
We first found Cheltenham sublime.

Ah, how the trivial would enchant!
	On our Botanic Gardens walk
We touched the tender Sensitive Plant
	And saw the fronds enfold the stalk
At each light blow our fingers dealt –
So very like ourselves, we felt.

But in the end they sent me down
	From that sweet hothouse world of bells
And crumbling walls of golden-brown
	And dotty peers and incense-smells
And dinners at the George and hock
And Wytham Woods and Godstow Lock.

Failed in Divinity! Oh count the hours
Spent on my knees in Cowley, Pusey House,
St. Barnabas', St. Mary Mag's, St. Paul's,
Revering chasubles and copes and albs!
Consider what I knew of 'High' and 'Low' . . .
Failed in Divinity! O, towers and spires!
Could no one help? Was nothing to be done?
No. No one. Nothing. Mercilessly calm,
The Cherwell carried under Magdalen Bridge
Its leisured puntfuls of the fortunate
Who next term and the next would still come back.

Could no one help? I'd seen myself a don,
Reading old poets in the library,
Attending chapel in an M.A. gown
And sipping vintage port by candlelight.
I sought my tutor in his arid room,
Who told me, "You'd have only got a Third."
I wandered into Blackwell's, where my bill
Was so enormous that it wasn't paid
Till ten years later, from the small estate
My father left. Not even dusty shelves
Of folios of architectural plates
Could comfort me. Outside, the sunny Broad,
The mouldering busts round the Sheldonian,
The hard Victorian front of Exeter,
The little colleges that front the Turl,
The lean acacia tree in Trinity,
Stood strong and confident, outlasting me.

Blackwell's Bookshop.

The Sheldonian
.'.The mouldering busts'.

I called on Ava. He was packing up
For Ireland, for the scintillating lake,
His gate-lodge, woods and winding avenue
Around the limestone walls of Clandeboye.
"Cheer up! You're looking like a soul in hell.
Here's some Amontillado." As I drank,
Already I could hear my father's voice.
"My boy, henceforward your allowance stops:
You'll copy me, who with my strong right arm
Alone have got myself the victory."
"Your father's right, John; you must earn your keep."
Pentonville Road! How could I go by tram
In suit from Savile Row and Charvet tie?
How could I, after Canterbury Quad,
My peers and country houses and my jokes,
Talk about samples, invoices and stock?

137

Ah, welcome door, Gabbitas Thring & Co.'s
Scholastic agency in Sackville Street!
"The Principal will see you." "No degree?
There is, perhaps, a temporary post
As cricket master for the coming term
As Gerrard's Cross. Fill in this form and give
Qualifications – testimonials
Will help – and if you are accepted, please
Pay our commission promptly. Well, good day!"

The sun that shone on Edward James
    Shone also down on me –
A prep-school master teaching Games,
    Maths, French, Divinity.
Harsh hand-bells harried me from sleep
For thirty pounds a term and keep.

And he continued friendly still,
    And wrote his verses out with care
On vellum with a coloured quill,
    And published them in volumes rare
Of hand-made paper bound up fine . . .
And then, by Jove, he published mine!

They tell me he's in Mexico,
    They will not give me his address;
But if he sees this book he'll know
    I do not value him the less.
For Art is long and Life must end,
My earlier publisher and friend.

CRICKET MASTER
      (*An Incident*)

My undergraduate eyes beholding,
      As I climbed your slope, Cat Hill:
Emerald chestnut fans unfolding,
      Symbols of my hope, Cat Hill.
What cared I for past disaster,
Applicant for cricket master,
Nothing much of cricket knowing,
Conscious but of money owing?
      Somehow I would cope, Cat Hill.

"The sort of man we want must be prepared
To take our first eleven. Many boys
From last year's team are with us. You will find
Their bowling's pretty good and they are keen."
"And so am I, Sir, very keen indeed."
Oh where's mid-on? And what is silly point?
Do six balls make an over? Help me, God!
"Of course you'll get some first-class cricket too;
The MCC send down an A team here."
My bluff had worked. I sought the common-room,
Of last term's pipe-smoke faintly redolent.
It waited empty with its worn arm-chairs
For senior bums to mine, when in there came
A fierce old eagle in whose piercing eye
I saw that instant-registered dislike
Of all unhealthy aesthetes such as me.
"I'm Winters – you're our other new recruit
And here's another new man – Barnstaple."
He introduced a thick Devonian.

"Let's go and have some practice in the nets.
You'd better go in first." With but one pad,
No gloves, and knees that knocked in utter fright,
Vainly I tried to fend the hail of balls
Hurled at my head by brutal Barnstaple
And at my shins by Winters. Nasty quiet
Followed my poor performance. When the sun
Had sunk behind the fringe of Hadley Wood
And Barnstaple and I were left alone
Among the ash-trays of the common-room,
He murmured in his soft West-country tones:
"D'you know what Winters told me, Betjeman?
He didn't think you'd ever held a bat."

    The trusting boys returned. "We're jolly glad
You're on our side, Sir, in the trial match."
"But I'm no good at all." "Oh yes, you are."
When I was out first ball, they said "Bad luck!
You hadn't got your eye in." Still I see
Barnstaple's smile of undisguised contempt,
Still feel the sting of Winters' silent sneer.
Disgraced, demoted to the seventh game,
Even the boys had lost their faith in me.
God guards his aesthetes. If by chance these lines
Are read by one who in some common-room
Has had his bluff called, let him now take heart:
In every school there is a sacred place
More holy than the chapel. Ours was yours:
I mean, of course, the first-eleven pitch.
Here in the welcome break from morning work,
The heavier boys, of milk and biscuits full,

Sat on the roller while we others pushed
Its weighty cargo slowly up and down.
We searched the grass for weeds, caressed the turf,
Lay on our stomachs squinting down its length
To see that all was absolutely smooth.

     The prize-day neared. And, on the eve before,
We masters hung our college blazers out
In readiness for tomorrow. Matron made
A final survey of the boys' best clothes –
Clean shirts. Clean collars. "Rice, your jacket's torn.
Bring it to me this instant!" Supper done,
Barnstaple drove his round-nosed Morris out
And he and I and Vera Spencer-Clarke,
Our strong gymnasium mistress, squashed ourselves
Into the front and rattled to The Cock.

     Sweet bean-fields then were scenting Middlesex;
Narrow lanes led between the dairy-farms
To ponds reflecting weather-boarded inns.
There on the wooden bench outside The Cock
Sat Barnstaple, Miss Spencer-Clarke and I,
At last forgetful of tomorrow's dread
And gazing into sky-blue Hertfordshire.
Three pints for Barnstaple, three halves for me,
Sherry of course for Vera Spencer-Clarke.

     Pre-prize-day nerves? Or too much bitter beer?
What had that evening done to Barnstaple?
I only know that singing we returned;
The more we sang, the faster Barnstaple
Drove his old Morris, swerving down the drive
And in and out the rhododendron clumps,

Over the very playing-field itself,
And then – oh horror! – right across the pitch
Not once, but twice or thrice. The mark of tyres
Next day was noticed at the Parents' Match.
That settled Barnstaple and he was sacked,
While I survived him, lasting three more terms.

Shops and villas have invaded
    Your chestnut quiet there, Cat Hill.
Cricket field and pitch degraded,
    Nothing did they spare, Cat Hill.
Vera Spencer-Clarke is married
And the rest are dead and buried;
I am thirty summers older,
Richer, wickeder and colder,
    Fuller too of care, Cat Hill.